# Spirit Animals

*Modern Guides to Ancient Wisdom*

HERRON

# Contents

# Introduction

—

*Open your heart and mind to the wisdom
and guidance of your spirit animal, and you will
have a trusted companion by your side.*

If you think about it, certain animals have always been there with you – in childhood, perhaps you eagerly patted a passing puppy, begged your parents for a bunny rabbit, or simply wondered at a buzzy bee or butterfly. In adulthood, you may have your own pet, or enjoy interactions with animals on walks in nature, or looking at them from the office window. There are animals that you are drawn to, most obviously because you like them, or perhaps they pop up frequently, manifest in your dreams, or linger in your memory more than others. If you learn to tune in, you will discover that these animals have much to teach you.

All it takes is a little leap of faith. Was that a chance encounter or a message from your animal guide? You get to decide. In the opening pages of this book, you will learn some simple techniques to help you summon your spirit animal and learn how to travel with them on your life's journey. The spirit animal profiles, listed in alphabetical order for ease of reference, provide information about the symbolism of each animal, what it may be trying to teach you and, importantly, practical ways for how you can respond if you feel this animal is your guide.

Don't miss the opportunity to enrich your inner world and feel the security, companionship and wisdom of having a spirit animal by your side as you navigate your way in this life.

# Summon your spirit animal

—

*Channelling your spirit animal sounds like a mighty task involving a lot of chimes and crystals (and, yes, these can help), but why not start with a simple question. What animal do you feel a strong connection with? Keep that question in mind as you travel on this journey.*

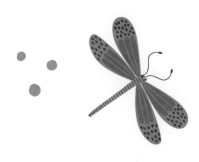

## THINK ABOUT IT

Your spirit guide may seem like a symbolic representation of yourself, so first: consider yourself. Are you a leader or follower, introvert or extrovert, active or sedentary, creative or practical, quick witted or open hearted?

Flick back through your life. What animals have you been drawn to? Which have you kept as a pet or always wanted to? Are there any animals that have appeared regularly throughout your life, or that just strike an unshakable chord with you.

Once you have considered these questions, spend some time researching those particular animals. Use this book for research or as a prompt to discover which animals jibe with your attributes, energy and memories.

## JOURNAL MEDITATION

If you are serious about calling in your spirit animal, you'll want to prioritise this practice. Do it daily.

Prepare for your meditation in a calm, uncluttered space. Make sure you have a pen and journal to hand. Place a crystal in your meditation space if you would like to.

Set an intention that you wish to connect with your spirit animal. Be as clear and direct as you can, and find language that works for you.

Close your eyes and begin to take deep breaths in and out. On the out breath, repeat your intention – you can speak it out loud or within. Continue this practice of breathing while focussing on your intention. Be patient and wait for contact with your spirit animal.

At the end of your practice, write down in your journal all of your observations. Be as specific as you can. Make note of the environment, recording the colours, shapes and objects you see. Record the animal(s) that appeared to you and what they were doing. Try to recall any emotional context – the feeling you got from the animal or how you were feeling. Set the journal aside.

After a few hours have passed, you can read your notes. In time, you will notice elements that repeat in your meditation, and by reflecting deeply on what you observe, you will be uncovering the deeper layers within yourself – thanks to the wisdom of the spirit animal at your side.

If your spirit animal does not appear in meditation, remain positive. Simply try again later and keep trying until you are successful. It will happen.

Note: You may wish to modify this meditation by focussing on a specific animal, perhaps one that has come to you during the thinking process outlined earlier. You might invite this animal into your meditation by way of a drawing, photograph or figurine. During meditation, focus on the lessons this animal may be trying to teach you. Again write them down and review later. You can repeat this exercise with different animals and compare your notes to identify what resonates most with you.

### LOOK TO YOUR DREAMS

Our dreams (and daydreams) provide valuable glimpses into our subconscious, that fertile inner landscape which controls so much of our brain power but can remain a mystery. Messages from our unconscious via dreams are like gold dust, helping illuminate our spiritual pathway.

Keep a journal by your bedside. When you wake up after an active dream, be sure to note down any objects, symbols, colours or feelings you experienced. Make particular note if an animal appeared to you. Keep on doing this and review regularly, looking for connections and messages that may be coming your way from your spirit animal.

## GO FOR A WALK

Put on your sneakers and leave behind your phone, and get out into nature for a walk. While you are walking, look and listen to the sights and sounds around you. Listen
to your thoughts too. Is there an animal that appears in your mind, or in physical form while you are walking? Is that an animal that you hope to see? Repeat this practice regularly and consider if the same animal reappears.

## CONSULT WITH AN INTUITIVE

Shamanic energy healers may be able to help you connect with your spirit animal. It takes a leap of faith but if you are open to drums, rattles, rocks, songs and plants being used to tap into your deeper consciousness then this is one way of meeting your spirit animal. A tarot reading may also help to point you in the right direction.

## GO ONLINE

A little less 'out there', but still worth doing, there are many online sites that offer quizzes to help you discover your spirit animal, as well as advice on techniques that you can use to get connected.

# Become your spirit animal

—

*To fully benefit from the relationship you have with your spirit animal, you must learn to view the world from their perspective.*

You must learn as much as you can about your spirit animal. Research and educate yourself about how the animal thinks, feels, moves, operates and lives in its world.

Inhabit your animal as fully and physically as possible. Find a place where you think your animal would feel comfortable and safe, and spend time there in meditation or reflection. Immerse yourself in your animal's natural habitat and endeavour to see the world through its eyes, and not your own. Crouch down, gallop, crawl, climb, do as your animal would do.

The learnings you glean will provide insights for your own life. Sift gently through your learnings. What insights stay caught in the net? These might be viewed as special powers – the energy and message of your spirit animal distilled.

With this understanding, you can move into the next phase of understanding that you too may hold this power. And that if you interact with your spirit animal appropriately, they will help you to learn and grow in this power, and release energy that will help you fulfil your life and soul's purpose.

To deepen the connection you have with your animal, and to maximise the lessons you can learn from it, meditate regularly and preferably at the same time each day so that your animal can meet you there. Follow the process on page 7, but you can replace with a specific intention or question that you would like to ask your animal. Remember to record your observations and review them at a later date.

# Journeying with your spirit animal

—

*Walk with your spirit animals and learn how they can guide you through the material and spiritual worlds.*

You can identify your one spirit animal and find that the journey stops there. But for many people, and historically, it is common to have multiple spirit guides. Each animal has something specific to teach us about ourselves and guidance to offer at a given moment when it is needed. If multiple animals appear in your life, it is important to maintain and nurture your relationship with each of them.

Many cultures believe that a single animal which stays with you for life, and with which you have a very strong connection, is your totem animal. This animal embodies the traits that you, in time, will also learn to manifest – for they are within you. This can be represented symbolically by way of a talisman, crest or piece of jewellery that you can wear to keep your magical animal close.

It is believed that each of us has nine animal spirits or essences that stand beside us, guiding us through this life. They are situated in certain positions. Four of them represent the directions north, south, east and west, while one sits above, one below and one within you. The remaining two animals walk either side of you.

Your guide in the east leads you in the spiritual dimensions of your life.

Your guide in the west leads you in the discovery of self-knowledge.

Your guide in the north reminds you to live in gratitude, and teaches when to listen and when to speak.

Your guide in the south protects your inner child.

Your guide above you connects you to the universe and the stars from which you came and to which you will return.

Your guide below helps you to stay connected with Mother Earth and grounded on your journey.

Your guide within protects your heart space and supports you to follow your dreams.

Your guide on the right is male energy which protects you like a father and gives you strength.

Your guide on the left is female energy which nurtures you and teaches you to love and be loved.

# Find your
# spirit animal

—

*Discover the symbolism and ancient
wisdom of these animals and how they can help
protect and guide you on life's journey.*

# Alpaca

*Embody confidence and dignity*

**ESSENCE** *Wisdom, power and adaptability*

## SYMBOLISM

- Courage and stamina
- A long journey ahead
- Resilience in adversity
- Spiritual growth
- Focus and durability

## TEACHINGS

Alpaca as teacher brings the message that you have the tenacity and drive to overcome whatever life throws at you – and the courage to stand up for yourself when needed. Alpaca will help you find your personal power and show you how to overcome any challenges in your path.

## HOW TO RESPOND

**Move** forward by not dwelling on past failures or mistakes.

**Feel** empowered to stand up for yourself and speak the truth.

**Think** of the best ways to use your energy; slow and steady often wins the race.

**Look** to old dreams and projects, as this might be the time to resurrect them.

**Ask** yourself the difficult questions. Are you taking on too much? Do you need to set some boundaries? Do the inner work necessary to progress on your journey.

## MESSAGE

*Remember that you're adaptable and strong. These days will pass, and you'll be proud of what you achieved.*

# Ant

*Forge a new path to success*

**ESSENCE** *Strength, cooperation and guidance*

## SYMBOLISM

- Difficult choices
- Prosperity and wealth
- New opportunities on the horizon
- Good fortune
- New, exciting friendships

## TEACHINGS

When Ant appears, prepare to see movement and change. Ant is a trailblazer who is here to guide you to the next stage of your life path, bringing with him significant opportunities and personal growth. This will be a test of your strength and your commitment to the future you.

## HOW TO RESPOND

**Create** a vision board or a sacred space where you can manifest your dreams and start to make them a reality.

**Get organised** by decluttering your home and cutting off any toxic or negative relationships so you're ready for your new life ahead.

**Embrace** new situations and let go of past resistance or trauma.

**Find** people with the same goals and values as you, and work cooperatively with them.

**Slow down** and don't be impetuous. Patience, planning and hard work will see you reap true rewards.

## MESSAGE

*Prepare for a life-changing opportunity and trust in your ability to make it happen.*

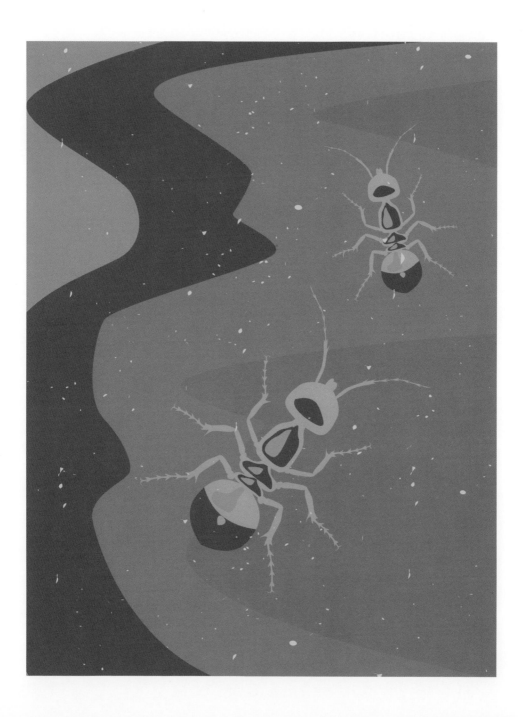

# Bat

*Seek the truth in all things*

ESSENCE *Perception, transformation and camouflage*

## SYMBOLISM

- Prophecy and psychic ability
- Removal of toxicity
- Inner soul work
- Spiritual growth
- Sacred moon magic

## TEACHINGS

Bat is a shapeshifter who teaches us to embrace transformation. When Bat comes into your life, he brings the gift of perception and the ability to observe unseen. Through his teachings you will understand how to face the darkness and move into the light in order to reach your full potential.

## HOW TO RESPOND

**Listen** to your dreams. The answers you seek will be in there if you look hard enough.

**Gaze** at the moon. Draw on her energy and her wisdom, and follow her cycles of renewal and rebirth.

**Journey** deep into your soul through self-inquiry to find your inner truth.

**Act** on new ideas, even if you don't know where they will lead. The journey of finding out will be part of your transformation.

**Be wary** of illusion and trickery. Meditation will ground you and help you focus on the truth.

## MESSAGE

*Do not fear change: your metamorphosis will come from a place of truth and wisdom.*

Your potential
is endless. Go do
what you were
created to do.

# Bear

*Harness the power of your full potential*

ESSENCE *Strength, solitude and protection*

## SYMBOLISM

- Arrival of a wise teacher
- Promotion or pay rise
- Warrior spirit
- New-found independence
- Shamanic healing

## TEACHINGS

When Bear comes into your life, it's a sign that you're being called on to step up and take decisive action. You will need to lead, but also be a pillar of support for others. Do not forget that Bear is a shaman, and you may need to call on your healing powers.

## HOW TO RESPOND

**React** decisively and confidently. Trust your instincts and face challenges head on.

**Stand up** for your beliefs and use your charisma to convince others.

**Direct** your energy carefully. You may need to set boundaries to ensure you are not drained of life force.

**Find** comfort in solitude. Like Bear, learn to seek out quiet spaces and be content in your own company.

**Provide** strength and support to others, and be generous in sharing your wisdom.

## MESSAGE

*Draw on all your life experiences to find the strength and courage you need.*

# Beetle

*Accept change with grace and fortitude*

**ESSENCE** *Rebirth, trust and integrity*

## SYMBOLISM

- The gift of clairvoyance
- Nurturing and healing
- New possibilities
- Inner strength
- Omen of good fortune

## TEACHINGS

Beetle teaches that we walk the same paths over and over again and that true power is found in creating a new route to a better life. It may be time to admit that you need to make some changes in order to be true to your core self.

## HOW TO RESPOND

**Delve** deep into your past actions and words as this is where your metamorphosis will begin.

**Focus** on your health, both mental and physical. This is the time to both harness your inner strength and nurture your inner child.

**Use** affirmations to overcome self-sabotaging and negative thoughts and help shift your mindset.

**Seek** out the sun. You will be able to see your opportunities more clearly in the bright light of day.

**Trust** your instincts and rely on your ability to survive and adapt.

## MESSAGE

*Use your intuition to understand where change is needed in your life, and act accordingly.*

# Bowerbird

*Open yourself up to new love*

**ESSENCE** *Romance, colour and gregariousness*

## SYMBOLISM

- A creative project
- Grace and self-acceptance
- Positivity
- A new love match
- Home improvements or renovation

## TEACHINGS

Bowerbird reminds us of the patience, dedication and focus needed for true artistry. When Bowerbird comes to you, listen to his joyous lessons of creativity and generosity. He is teaching you to celebrate your gifts and that you are worthy of love just as you are.

## HOW TO RESPOND

**Be grateful** for the small things in life. Celebrate romance and friendship, and always treat people with care and respect.

**Revel** in your ability to create a harmonious, happy home full of love and laughter. It is a true blessing.

**See** yourself as worthy. Receive love and gifts with gratitude and grace.

**Be selective** and only collect objects that you love and do not put too much value on material things. Your attitude is more important than what you own.

**Create** your ideal life. Follow your heart instead of the crowds.

## MESSAGE

*When you follow your passions, you will be rewarded with true love, happiness and contentment.*

What if the change that you are avoiding is the one that gives you wings?

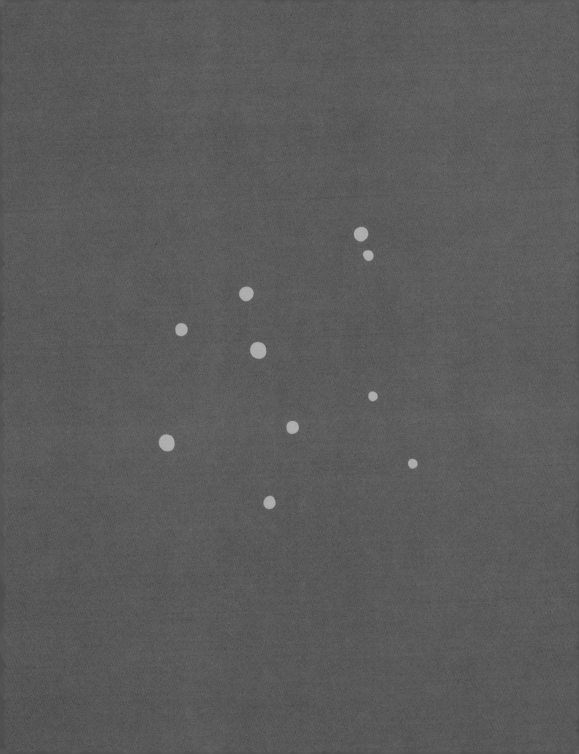

# Butterfly
## Transform with lightness and grace

ESSENCE *Change, joy and colour*

### SYMBOLISM

- Personal transformation
- Transition through life cycles
- Renewal, rebirth
- Lightness of being
- The human psyche

### TEACHINGS

Butterfly as a teacher puts great emphasis on movement: the smooth flow from one state to another. When the butterfly comes into your life as spirit guide, change is on the horizon. It may be time to let go of somebody or something that has been holding you back.

### HOW TO RESPOND

**Simplify** and go back to the little things and tend to them like flowers.

**Pause** and take a deep breath; a shift in perspective may be all that is needed.

**Be present** and live in the moment. Inhale the sweet nectar of Now.

**Look** within and consider ways to release your fears and surrender to love.

**Act** but don't rush. Slow, mindful changes are more likely to be longer-lasting. Your inner butterfly will emerge from its work when the time is right.

### MESSAGE

*Tune into areas in your life or personality that are in need of change or transformation.*

# Camel

## Seek guidance through a difficult situation

**ESSENCE** *Strength, endurance and accomplishment*

### SYMBOLISM

- A spiritual pilgrimage
- Good health
- New adventures and opportunities
- Strong work ethic
- Resistance to change

### TEACHINGS

When Camel comes into your life, it is a sign that you are on a path to success and prosperity. The road may be tough at times, but you have the endurance and stamina to succeed. Camel will guide you to the riches that you deserve, both material and spiritual.

### HOW TO RESPOND

**Look** ahead and don't veer off course. Be clear in the path and destination you have chosen.

**Be prepared** to encounter obstacles and pitfalls. Like Camel, you will be travelling through some of the harshest terrain imaginable to reach your oasis.

**Stay** positive as this attitude will see you through any tough times.

**Be adaptable** as life may take you in a very different direction, and you must embrace that fearlessly.

**Remain** clear headed as significant financial gain may seem like a reward, but it can bring its own challenges.

### MESSAGE

*Abundance will be coming your way. Know that you are on the right path for success.*

# Cat

*Trust your instincts when making big decisions*

**ESSENCE** *Independence, curiosity and communication*

## SYMBOLISM

- Renewed perspective
- Dark magic
- Connection to the spirit world
- Work-life balance
- Psychic energy

## TEACHINGS

Cat as teacher brings the message that you must seek out quiet so you are able to listen carefully. Someone from the spirit world is trying to deliver a message, and you need to trust your intuition on how to proceed. Like Cat, you must always be selective and astute.

## HOW TO RESPOND

**Seek** out nature and wild places. It is here that you will be able to best communicate with the spirit and astral realms.

**Look** for patterns, symbols and other signs in the world around you. Use these to guide your thoughts and actions.

**Investigate** chakra healing, with a focus on balancing your third eye chakra.

**Find** solitude in the darkness of night. Like Cat, use this time to seek out intrigue.

**Believe** in yourself. You will know what to do when the time comes.

## MESSAGE

*Be watchful for new signs. An important message is coming that you need to heed.*

# Caterpillar

## Find liberation from the past

**ESSENCE** *Patience, endurance and determination*

## SYMBOLISM

- New opportunities on the horizon
- Spiritual rebirth
- Surrender to transformation
- Creative inspiration
- Personal growth

## TEACHINGS

Just as Caterpillar knows that he will at some point transform, so will you. You are now on a path to a new life; stay focussed, embrace your fears and trust the process. Caterpillar teaches you to remain humble in the knowledge that one day you will soar high.

## HOW TO RESPOND

**Break** out of your cocoon and manifest your new life. It's time to free yourself from negative energies and thought processes.

**Create** a mantra that reinforces what you're hoping to achieve. Chant these words each morning.

**Watch** out for dangers in your path and keep deceitful and untrustworthy people at bay.

**Remember** the importance of patience. You can't force change; it may arrive when you least expect it.

**Evolve** with grace and humility. Your journey is no more or less important than anyone else's.

## MESSAGE

*Great changes are coming your way and you must prepare so you are ready for them.*

# If I try to be like them, who will be like me?

*Yiddish Proverb*

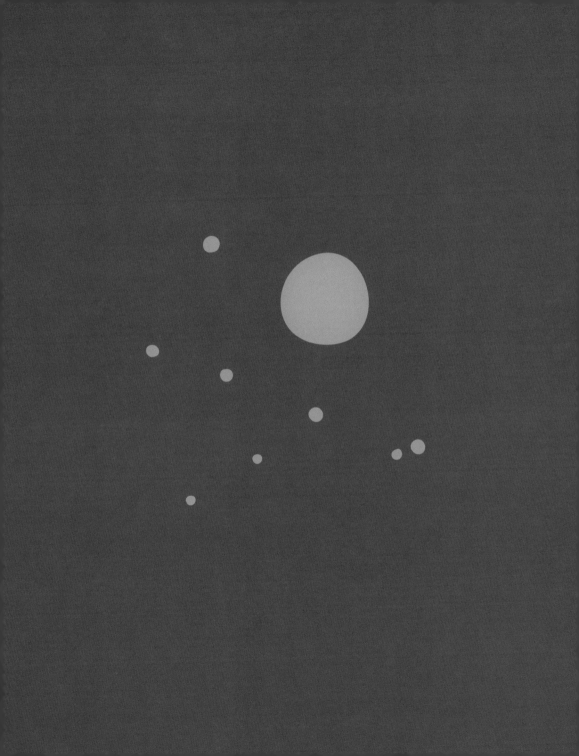

# Chameleon

*Be proud to show your true self*

---

**ESSENCE** *Disguise, focus and clairvoyance*

---

## SYMBOLISM

- Summoning change
- Exploration of new truths
- Versatility and adaptability
- Casting off old relationships
- Shape-shifting and sorcery

## TEACHINGS

When Chameleon comes into your life, this is a sign that you are ready to be noticed. Although you have always been a master of disguise, now is the time to show your true colours. Stop blending into the background, and don't let anything stand in your way.

## HOW TO RESPOND

**Dig** deep and find your courage. It's time to break free and explore your passions.

**Remember** that although you're well-practised in hiding your emotions, freedom comes when you show your authentic self.

**Be prepared** for a new job, a new project or a new relationship. It's essential to make the right choices now so you are set up for the future.

**Have** faith that you will succeed. You are lucky that you are versatile and can easily adapt to all situations.

**Remember** that along with rewards come greater responsibilities.

---

## MESSAGE

*It's time to step out of your comfort zone and focus on your ultimate goals.*

# Clownfish

## Keep your friends and family close

**ESSENCE** *Beauty, companionship and faith*

### SYMBOLISM

- Co-dependence
- A luxurious lifestyle
- Joy in authentic connection
- Hidden dangers and obstacles
- Strength of character

### TEACHINGS

Just as Clownfish happily survives in a symbiotic relationship with Anemone, you too must find your tribe in order to reach your full potential. When Clownfish appears as spirit animal, he teaches that greater happiness can be found when you share your triumphs and celebrate your wins with the people around you.

### HOW TO RESPOND

**Allow** your friends to support you through difficult times, and provide support and guidance when they are in need.

**Stop** hiding from challenging or difficult situations, and don't be afraid to take risks. You are braver than you think.

**Practise** mindfulness in order to cultivate a state of non-judgement.

**Remember** that suffering, loss and failure are all part of being human and similar experiences are shared by others.

**Work on** your insecurities. Otherwise you will always need the love and approval of other people to feel good about yourself.

### MESSAGE

*Before you seek out members of your tribe, it's important to truly know yourself first.*

# Cockatoo

## Communicate your desires to the world

**ESSENCE** *Intelligence, beauty and loyalty*

## SYMBOLISM

- Strong community ties
- Monogamy and lifelong companionship
- A new dawn
- Emotional vulnerability
- Self-care and self-love

## TEACHINGS

When Cockatoo flaps his wings, he brings the message of loyalty and love. If you follow his teachings, light will come into a dark situation and you will find hope on the horizon. Like Cockatoo, place value on teamwork and cooperation; allow yourself to be lifted up by the strength of others.

## HOW TO RESPOND

**Prepare** yourself for significant change. Remember that positive thoughts lead to positive outcomes.

**Find** compromise in your relationships. Like the seasons of the year, change is ongoing and balance is always shifting.

**Remember** to look behind the facade to see the truths buried deep within the soul.

**Improve** your body language. If you learn how to best present yourself to the world, the rewards can be profound.

**Develop** more self-awareness. Mindfulness, meditation and introspection are all useful tools for you to master.

## MESSAGE

*Be spontaneous and fearless in your endeavours. Your charisma and self-belief will take you far.*

# Never trust your fears. They don't know your strength.

*Athena Singh*

# Cougar

*Take action when the time is right*

---

**ESSENCE** *Elegance, grace and courage*

---

## SYMBOLISM

- A messenger of change
- Divine feminine energy
- Influential leadership
- New chances
- Stealth and power

## TEACHINGS

Cougar as spirit animal teaches that it is possible to lead with fairness and grace, and that power does not have to be about control or dominion over others. Everything in the universe has an opposite: this is what allows us to experience life to the fullest and appreciate the good in the world.

## HOW TO RESPOND

**Protect** what is precious to you by keeping harmful people and situations at arm's length.

**Leap** into all opportunities that are presented to you. This is your time to shine and actions can sometimes speak louder than words.

**Set** clear intentions and strong boundaries. You have chosen your path; now stick to it.

**Lead** by example. You have great power and must use it wisely. Humility, empathy and fairness are all attributes of great rulers.

**Identify** your areas of weakness and work on them diligently.

---

## MESSAGE

*Harness your inner strength as you are destined for great things in the future.*

# Coyote

*Stay one step ahead of the pack*

**ESSENCE** *Adaptability, intelligence and chaos*

## SYMBOLISM

- A spirit of resourcefulness
- Keeper of magic
- The joker
- Trickery and deceit
- Sense of humour

## TEACHINGS

Just as Coyote is a cunning and clever animal, he teaches that you too must be savvy in your approach to life. When Coyote appears as spirit animal, know that you may be about to encounter a difficult person or situation, and that you will need your wits about you to emerge unscathed.

## HOW TO RESPOND

**Rethink** your perspective on a situation that is troubling you.

**Listen** carefully, as there may be a hidden meaning behind the words you're hearing.

**Know** that you are in possession of a deep wisdom. The answers you need will come to you when you slow down.

**Remember** that there's a fine line between playfulness and chaos. Keep things light and don't get bogged down in drama.

**Seek out** the root cause of physical, emotional or psychological distress. Only then will you be able to overcome it.

## MESSAGE

*Be wary of trickery or subterfuge – someone may be trying to bring you down.*

# Crab

## Change your direction in life

**ESSENCE** *Resilience, adventure and protection*

### SYMBOLISM

- The cyclical nature of life
- Rebirth and resurrection
- Moon wisdom
- Unexpected opportunities
- Travel to distant shores

### TEACHINGS

Crab as teacher comes to show you your new path through the world. Just as Crab scuttles sideways on the sand, be prepared to move in an unexpected direction in the near future. Although this may not have been part of your plan, don't be apprehensive: you are ready to take on a big adventure.

### HOW TO RESPOND

**Harness** the energy of the full moon through journalling, meditating or charging your crystals.

**Nurture** yourself through the period of instability. Until you are comfortable in your new environment, be sure to put your needs first.

**Stop** procrastinating and consider taking action. You cannot stay in your shell forever.

**Look** for new ways to express your ideas and emotions to others. Sometimes the best solutions can be the most unconventional.

**Be brave** as any changes to your life will improve it for the better. There's no need for concern.

### MESSAGE

*Surrender and let the situation unfold. There are things that you have no control over.*

I've never seen any life transformation that didn't begin with the person in question finally getting tired of their own bullshit.

*Elizabeth Gilbert*

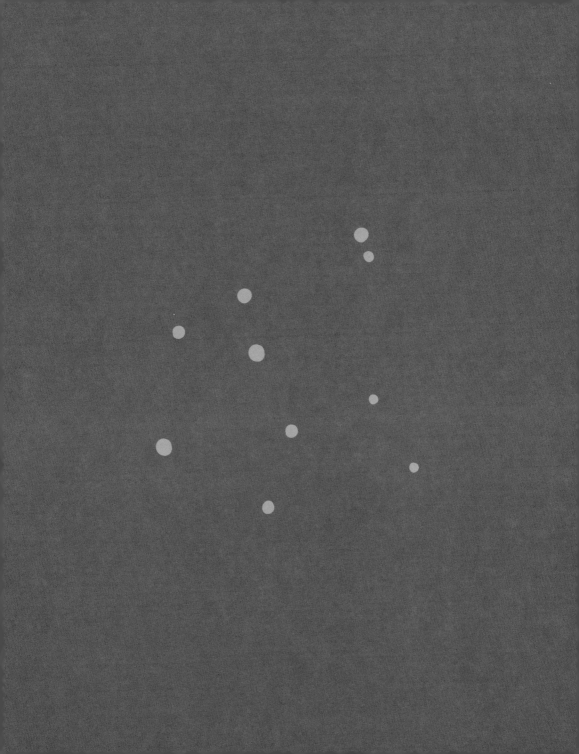

# Crocodile

*Be your authentic self at all times*

**ESSENCE** *Power, healing and freedom*

## SYMBOLISM

- New knowledge and wisdom
- Survival instinct
- Connection to Mother Earth
- Truth seeking
- A journey of self-discovery

## TEACHINGS

The ancient lineage of Crocodile brings with it the teachings of survival and growth. Crocodile reminds you that when you are your true self you can better self-advocate and stand up for what you need. Continue to work on embracing your emotions and building self-awareness to find inner peace.

## HOW TO RESPOND

**Take** back your power by establishing healthy boundaries and practising forgiveness.

**Look** for opportunities to acquire new knowledge and wisdom, such as through workshops, classes and sacred circles.

**Be aware** of your attitude. Although you are highly emotionally intelligent, sometimes your primal instincts can take over.

**Understand** your core values, needs and desires, and use this to choose a life path that fulfils you.

**Release** old habits, regrets and negative energies through a burning ceremony in order to focus on what is truly significant to you.

## MESSAGE

*Make a conscious choice to stand out from the crowd and dare to be different.*

# Crow

## Move forward with confidence and clarity

**ESSENCE** *Destiny, reflection and wisdom*

### SYMBOLISM

- Divine messages and omens
- The gift of forbearance
- New-found personal integrity
- Sacred laws
- Ancestral wisdom

### TEACHINGS

Crow represents creation and spiritual strength, and teaches that you have the wisdom of your ancestors behind you. Keep looking forward and be clear about your desires. When Crow comes into your life, you will know that you have chosen the right path and that you will not fail in your endeavours.

### HOW TO RESPOND

**Focus** on your journey which should now be straightforward, providing you maintain a clear vision.

**Be kind** as you have the opportunity to teach others and you should see this as a blessing.

**Reclaim** your spiritual heritage. Honour the memory of your ancestors in order to keep their spirits happy and at peace.

**Pay attention** to any new advice, omens or signs. These contain important messages about the next steps you must take.

**Be mindful** of your opinions and actions. Others are watching and learning from you.

### MESSAGE

*Don't stop – everything you have been working towards is now coming to fruition.*

# Deer

## *Extricate yourself from a difficult situation*

**ESSENCE** *Grace, gentleness and speed*

### SYMBOLISM

- A return to innocence
- Regeneration
- Harmony and unity
- Effective communication
- A shift in perspective

### TEACHINGS

Deer brings the lesson of dealing with problems tactfully and gracefully. Deer as spirit animal teaches you to diplomatically remove yourself from stressful or difficult situations, leaving your spirit unburdened and your reputation untarnished. Work on being gracious and considerate in all matters and you will be blessed with improved relationships, harmonious friendships and career success.

### HOW TO RESPOND

**Act** with kindness and compassion at all times.

**Trust** your instincts, move fast and remain vigilant. Rely on your emotional intelligence to get you through situations.

**Analyse** your circumstances. Zero in on the problem and study all sides. What are the causes and how can you influence things for the better?

**Avoid stress** by examining your values and living by them. Your gentle soul is deeply affected by both internal and external conflict.

**Make** a plan as concrete steps toward something better will create a sense of progress.

### MESSAGE

*Although a problem may seem insurmountable, trust in your ability to smooth things over.*

# Dog

*Know yourself to be worthy of affection*

**ESSENCE** *Loyalty, love and devotion*

## SYMBOLISM

- A joyful approach to life
- Playfulness
- Trustworthiness and reliability
- Passion for justice
- Fear of abandonment

## TEACHINGS

Dog as teacher puts emphasis on being a faithful companion and loyal friend. When Dog comes into your life, a new love or friendship – or a shake-up of an old one – may be on the horizon. Prepare by working on self-love and acceptance, and step back from negative people and activities.

## HOW TO RESPOND

**Manifest** your ideal relationship by opening your mind and asking the universe for what you are looking for. Be clear and specific on the kind of person you wish to attract.

**Focus** on wellbeing and happiness. This is more important than financial or material success.

**Be present** so you are aware of the opportunities the universe throws your way.

**Regroup** with family when life gets tough. This is where you'll find true, unconditional love.

**Seek** joy and fun in all situations. Life is too short to always be serious.

## MESSAGE

*A new friendship or relationship is on the horizon that will shake up your life.*

# Dolphin

*See the good in all things*

**ESSENCE** *Intelligent, inquisitive and playful*

## SYMBOLISM

- Personal and spiritual rebirth
- Sense of humour
- Child-like wonder
- Balance and harmony
- Successful teamwork

## TEACHINGS

Dolphin as teacher brings the message that harmony in life is a blessing. By studying Dolphin's gentle nature, you will learn to see joy in all situations and bring new-found peace and positivity to those around you. Focus on diffusing tense situations and refraining from judgement in order to create joy in your life.

## HOW TO RESPOND

**Surround** yourself with positivity. This means you'll have an easier time seeing beauty in the world.

**Act** confidently even in the face of difficulties. Your attitude is as important as your actions.

**Think** about how you can best serve your community, perhaps through volunteering or helping a neighbour.

**Make** sure your words come from a place of selflessness and love. Just as Dolphin is a master communicator, you can make big changes with small words.

**Celebrate** how much we are all alike instead of focussing on our differences.

## MESSAGE

*Look for the positive intention behind every action. This will free you of the burden of judgement.*

# Taking no chances means wasting your dreams.

*Ellen Hopkins*

# Dove

*Embrace new opportunities without fear*

**ESSENCE** *Peace, purity and understanding*

## SYMBOLISM

- A restless spirit
- Compassion and kindness
- Message from a higher power
- Sacred unity
- A loyal guide

## TEACHINGS

If Dove has chosen to be your spirit animal, a new world is opening up to you that will cause a powerful and long-lasting shift in your life. Dove is a harbinger of spring and new beginnings; it's time to let go of whatever baggage you're holding onto and fly into the unknown.

## HOW TO RESPOND

**Organise** your life by purging your belongings, setting deadlines and writing lists. Don't let your clutter control you.

**Be proactive** and focus on your long-term vision and make personal development a priority for yourself.

**Prioritise** your home and your family. If you are on the path to parenthood, this might happen sooner than you think.

**Release** yourself from whatever is holding you back. You can only soar if you are free of burden.

**Indulge** in some self-care, stress relief and self-reflection. Few things flourish if neglected.

## MESSAGE

*Prepare yourself for a major life change. It's time to spread your wings and fly high.*

# Dragonfly

*Know that upheaval is in your future*

**ESSENCE** *Renewal, clarity and contentment*

## SYMBOLISM

- Surfacing of new desires
- Turning dreams into reality
- Self-realisation
- A spiritual evolution
- Bearer of light

## TEACHINGS

Just as Dragonfly flits between water and air, you too will move into a new situation in the near future. Dragonfly teaches that this is not something to be afraid of: you now have the skills to cope, and the outcome will bring you happiness and clarity in life.

## HOW TO RESPOND

**Focus** on the sensations in your body. Explore whether fear is fuelling you and stopping you from moving forward.

**Stop** procrastinating. You need to show up, do the work and keep aiming ever higher.

**Use** stones and crystals to purify and balance your chakras and dispel negativity from your life.

**Train** your mind to thrive on change. Be ready for unexpected twists and embrace imperfection.

**Look up** as all the possibilities in the world are around you – sometimes you just need to be looking the right way.

## MESSAGE

*There is no need to fear disruption: staying put is often riskier than changing.*

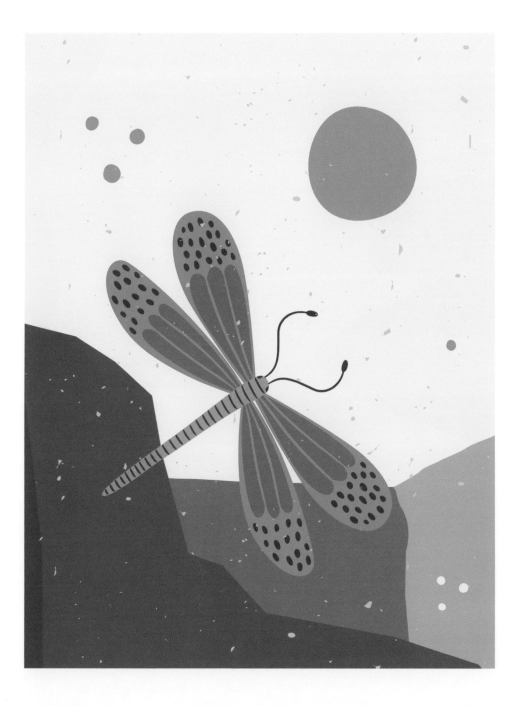

# Eagle

*Feel empowered to make decisions*

**ESSENCE** *Salvation, hope and pride*

## SYMBOLISM

- Clear vision
- An authoritarian figure
- A broad perspective on life
- Self-healing rituals
- A wise mentor

## TEACHINGS

When Eagle comes into your life, he brings the message that it may be time to take matters into your own hands. Eagle teaches that to rule the skies you need clear vision and strong judgement. Step back and get some perspective on the situation at hand, then act with courage, determination and confidence.

## HOW TO RESPOND

**Choose** your words carefully. How you deal with this matter will not be forgotten.

**Embark** on a journey of self-discovery. Rediscover who you are and search for meaning and purpose in your life.

**Bask** in solitude. You are a free spirit and you often need time alone to regenerate and regroup.

**Act** decisively. There's no need to draw the situation out, especially as people may be waiting on your verdict.

**Listen** to trusted outside perspectives. This is where you may find the answers you need.

## MESSAGE

*Use your new-found power wisely as the choices you make have the power to affect many.*

# Elephant
*Forgive with grace and courage*

**ESSENCE** *Strength, harmony and temperance*

## SYMBOLISM

- Beloved family member
- A call for help
- Sociability and charm
- A sense of duty
- Unique style

## TEACHINGS

Just as Elephant pays close attention to the wellbeing of his herd, it is time for you to take care of and protect those in a time of need. Perhaps a friend or family member needs support, or maybe you need help to face up to a tricky situation. There's nothing you can't get through together.

## HOW TO RESPOND

**Be prepared** to fight some battles. It's time to put yourself on the line to save a friendship.

**Exude** confidence and calm in all aspects of your life.

**Beware** of people trying to manipulate or take advantage of your kind nature. Stoke your inner power by confronting any issues head on.

**Embrace** and explore your feminine energy and turn to the sacred power of sisterhood for support.

**Nourish** yourself as you have a big journey in front of you and you need to build your strength.

## MESSAGE

*Do not forget that love and loyalty are important beyond all else in the world.*

The key to
keeping your
balance is
knowing when
you have lost it.

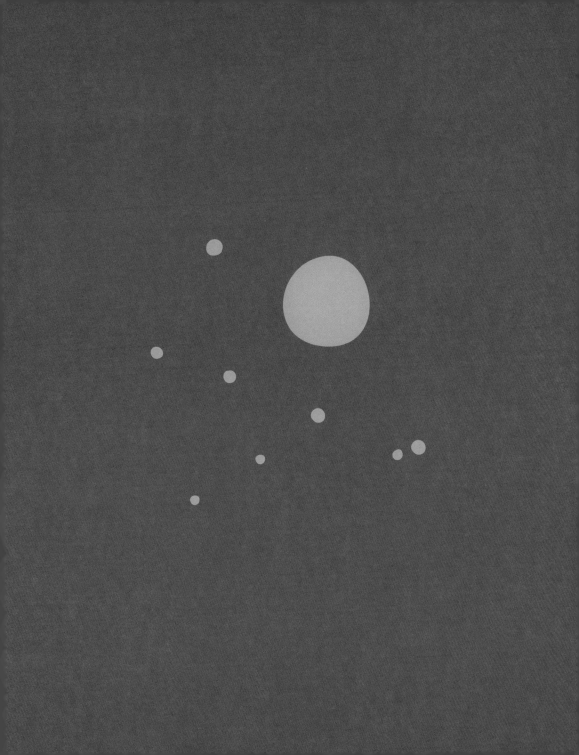

# Flamingo

*Regain balance in your life*

## SYMBOLISM

- Cooperative spirit
- Joyous nature
- New romance on the horizon
- Trust in fate
- Confidence to succeed

## TEACHINGS

When Flamingo comes into your life, it's time to decide what's important to you and what to jettison. Life offers infinite variety and it's easy to get lost in indecision with so many choices. To find balance, you need to direct your energies. Only then will you achieve your personal and professional goals.

## HOW TO RESPOND

**Visualise** your future. Ask yourself, 'What do I need to do in order for this to manifest in my life?' Set a timer and meditate on these words daily.

**Get tough** and decide what or who you need to cut out of your life in order to succeed.

**Identify** the most important people in your life and keep them close.

**Track** your thoughts by writing down how you feel. By doing this, you'll become aware of what might be standing in your way.

**Accept** that life is short and time is precious.

## MESSAGE

*Dream big! Success does not happen overnight, but it will start to happen when you're ready.*

# Fox
*Walk safely down your destined path*

**ESSENCE** *Intelligence, stealth and supremacy*

## SYMBOLISM

- A revered figure
- Guidance to a higher path
- Discerning nature
- The power of darkness
- Loneliness or seclusion

## TEACHINGS

When Fox is walking alongside you, know that you have the ability to see through deception and lies. Fox's appearance symbolises that it's time to carefully scan your surroundings as someone may be omitting important information or manipulating the truth. Be ready to face any subterfuge head on.

## HOW TO RESPOND

**Move** quickly through any obstacles in your path and find joy in your journey as it will result in great accomplishment and success.

**Stand** strong in the face of adversity and hold your head up high.

**Analyse** the facts. Often the truth is hidden in plain sight.

**Use** your instincts and creative energies to create the future you want on your own terms.

**Remember** that every problem has a solution. Dig deep and rely on your mental agility to find the resolution you desire.

## MESSAGE

*Although you may need to deal with a tricky situation, the outcome will be positive.*

# Frog
## *Look carefully at all the options*

**ESSENCE** *Fortitude, guidance and change*

## SYMBOLISM

- Fertility and abundance
- Connection to the spiritual realm
- Cleansing and renewal
- Emotional release
- Personal transformation

## TEACHINGS

Frog as spirit animal places great emphasis on being flexible in life. Just as Frog leaps between land and water, he teaches that you need to broaden your horizons and gain a new perspective. It may be time to look at your health or your career in a different way.

## HOW TO RESPOND

**Realise** the need for change. Without understanding the why, you won't be able to achieve your goals.

**Break** out of the ordinary and try something new, whether that's a hobby, a job or travels. Injecting fresh behaviours into your life will give you a boost.

**Ask** for help. See if a friend or trusted colleague has any new ideas.

**Overhaul** your routine. Change things up and see if that sparks your imagination.

**Pay attention** to the smallest details. These can make the difference between success and failure.

## MESSAGE

*Aim high and do everything in your power to become your best self.*

A rigid mind
is very sure but
often wrong.
A flexible mind is
generally unsure,
but often right.

*Vanda Scaravelli*

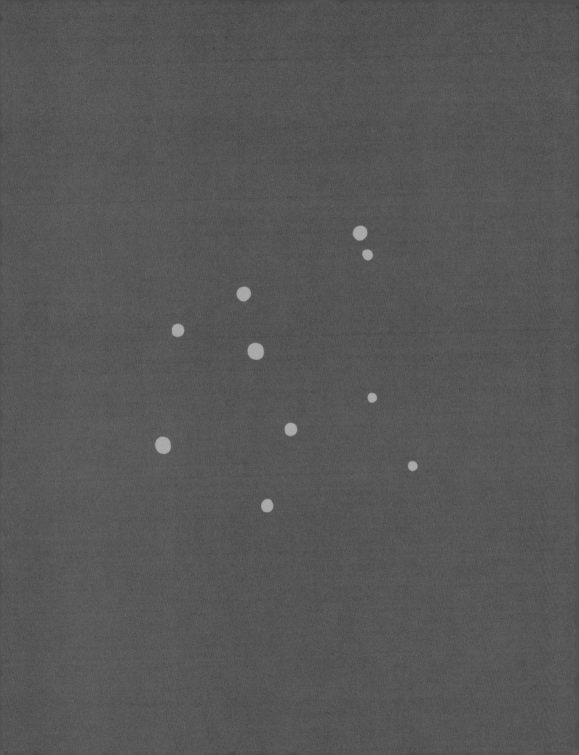

# Horse

*Express yourself freely and readily*

ESSENCE *Dependability, liberty and passion*

## SYMBOLISM

- Unexpected new adventures
- Masculine energy
- A pathway to freedom
- Mutual respect and honour
- Reaching your potential

## TEACHINGS

When Horse appears as spirit animal, he brings the message of galloping to freedom on distant horizons. By harnessing the animal's wild nature, you can use your drive and power to achieve whatever you want in life. Expect to soon find yourself on a wonderful new life phase or journey.

## HOW TO RESPOND

**Envisage** your wildest dreams and desires. Decide what it is that you want and start visualising that you are already there.

**Be empathic** as when you set off on new adventures, the resulting change can sometimes be difficult for others.

**Stay** motivated by regularly reviewing your goals and progress. Reward yourself for each milestone you reach.

**Rein in** runaway emotions and try to maintain your inner balance, stability and calm.

**Let go** of ideas that no longer serve you. It's time to look to the future.

## MESSAGE

*You are destined for big things if you can break free from your own constraints.*

# Hummingbird

*Find delight in every moment*

**ESSENCE** *Joy, colour and persistence*

## SYMBOLISM

- Lightness of being
- A playful nature
- The sweetness of life
- Messenger of hope
- Resilience and inner strength

## TEACHINGS

When tiny Hummingbird appears in your life, it's a sign that the sweet nectar of success is about to come your way. Hummingbird as spirit animal teaches that small actions can have big consequences and that your hard work will be justly rewarded. Be sure to share the accolades with everyone involved.

## HOW TO RESPOND

**Move** swiftly to grab the opportunities that will start coming your way.

**Bring** more colour into your life, whether that's through redecorating your home or reorganising your wardrobe.

**Move** your body as walking, a dance class or yoga will boost your mental and physical health and allow you to keep up with all of life's demands.

**Maintain** a positive outlook by writing in a gratitude journal each day.

**Enjoy** the simple things. Make time for family and friends, spend time in nature and get up early to watch the sunrise.

## MESSAGE

*To find true peace, surround yourself with love, integrity and honour at all times.*

# Iguana

*Embrace simplicity with gratitude*

**ESSENCE** *Patience, benevolence and understanding*

## SYMBOLISM

- Ancient wisdom
- The power of stillness
- Thoughtful observation
- Camouflage
- The healing power of the sun

## TEACHINGS

Iguana as spirit animal brings the message that you must learn to be content with what you have. Rather than striving for material success, seek out simpler pleasures. Take time to rest and recharge each day, and learn to live in the moment. Only then will you find true peace and happiness.

## HOW TO RESPOND

**Practise** meditation to reduce stress and increase concentration. This will also help you develop self-discipline and other beneficial habits.

**Donate** food, clothing, household goods and other items to people in need.

**Be genuine** in your actions. Forge your own path and speak your own mind, but always think about the potential effect on others.

**Work on** your self-esteem. Identify any negative beliefs you have about yourself, then challenge them.

**Stand back** and watch new situations unfold. You don't need to be swept up in drama.

## MESSAGE

*Always consider others and remember that a little kindness goes a long way.*

# Jaguar

*Boldly reclaim your inner power*

**ESSENCE** *Valour, ferocity and grace*

## SYMBOLISM

- Feminine power
- Ruler of the underworld
- The importance of self-reliance
- Beauty and youth
- Physical prowess

## TEACHINGS

Jaguar as spirit animal teaches that simplicity, contentment, acceptance and presence are hallmarks of an awakened life. When Jaguar appears, he is telling you that now is the time to look inwards. Only by doing this soul work can you clear any negative energies that may be impacting your daily life.

## HOW TO RESPOND

**Harness** the power of the night. Since your mind is most active after sunset, use this time to journal and meditate.

**Believe** in yourself. Adopt Jaguar's grace and confidence to make positive changes that are right for you.

**Use** the phases of the moon for guidance as you transition through each month.

**Choose** who you associate with wisely. Your successes are influenced by the people you surround yourself with.

**Learn** how to relax. Living in a prolonged state of high alert can be detrimental to your physical and mental health.

## MESSAGE

*It is crucial that you stay grounded and have faith in your ability to succeed.*

The more you
let go, the higher
you rise.

# Jellyfish
*Free yourself from perceived limitations*

**ESSENCE** *Fearlessness, surrender and transparency*

## SYMBOLISM

- Survival instinct
- Trust in a divine power
- Energetic flow
- Acceptance of fate
- A meditative state

## TEACHINGS

When Jellyfish appears as your spirit animal, you will learn to glide with the current and go with the flow. Jellyfish teaches that resistance to destiny is futile and that you must cultivate the ability to not only accept whatever comes, but embrace it too. It's time to let go and move on.

## HOW TO RESPOND

**Develop** the habit of looking at life through a positive mindset. Your attitude is everything.

**Immerse** yourself in water. This serves as a reminder of our natural human state: flowing, changing, self-aware and resilient.

**Let** events unfold naturally and accept that change will happen with or without you.

**Remove** negative people and influences from your life as they are just holding you back.

**Establish** balance in all areas of your life. Acknowledge that you have finite resources and that you cannot do everything all the time.

## MESSAGE

*Remember that the energy of surrender accomplishes much more than the energy of control.*

# Kangaroo
## *Boldly leap into the unknown*

**ESSENCE** *Balance, adaptation and independence*

## SYMBOLISM

- Spiritual enrichment
- Abundance of vigour and energy
- Strength of character
- Making wise choices
- Strong maternal instinct

## TEACHINGS

Kangaroo as teacher brings the message that if there are obstacles standing in the way of your dreams, now is the time to overcome them. Consider why these hurdles seem so insurmountable and who or what is sabotaging your efforts. It may be time to make some bold moves.

## HOW TO RESPOND

**Act** decisively by understanding what it will take to align your beliefs and your actions.

**Don't compare** yourself to others. Recognise that no one has your exact experiences and knowledge, all of which has led you to the path you're on.

**Use** your instinct to guide you away from unpleasant situations.

**Devote** yourself to personal and spiritual growth. Like Kangaroo, you must only move forwards, not backwards.

**Take** a leap of faith. You may not know exactly where you'll land, but launching yourself into the unknown can reap huge rewards.

## MESSAGE

*Do not fear the future – you have the innate ability to adapt to new situations.*

# Koala

*Be at peace with yourself*

**ESSENCE** *Co-dependence, empathy and security*

## SYMBOLISM

- New perspectives
- Strong tribal instincts
- Emotional release from past distress
- A happy, successful family
- Endless patience

## TEACHINGS

When Koala appears as your spirit animal, he brings a stern warning that you need to rest and recharge. Rather than racing through the journey of life, realise that your route is filled with beautiful scenery, wonderful people and interesting stops, if you can slow down enough to look.

## HOW TO RESPOND

**Make** your home your sanctuary by bringing in natural light and indoor plants.

**Manage** stress by learning and practising relaxation techniques. The fresh aroma of eucalyptus oil will provide calming relief at the start or end of your day.

**Change** your diet to include more plant-based meals.

**Indulge** in moments of calmness and relaxation. For the sake of your mental health, it is important to slot in a few minutes each day to decompress.

**Be** a valued member of your community. This will also increase your confidence and self-worth.

## MESSAGE

*Enjoy every rung on the ladder as you climb towards the stars.*

# Koi

## Expect career and financial success

**ESSENCE** *Wealth, perseverance and opportunity*

### SYMBOLISM

- Good luck charm
- Prosperity and harmony
- A successful career
- Restoration of peace
- The rewards of hard work

### TEACHINGS

Call on Koi as your spirit animal when you are stagnating at work and need a push in the right direction. Koi teaches that wealth and prosperity can be yours: you just need to be tenacious in achieving your goals. Put aside your pride and ego, and learn to swim with the current.

### HOW TO RESPOND

**Have** a purpose and a plan so you don't drift aimlessly through life.

**Reconnect** with old acquaintances and colleagues. This may bring about new opportunities and renewed friendships.

**Resurrect** unfinished creative projects or start new ones. Use boredom as creative fuel and breathe new life into your endeavours.

**Learn** to handle rejection, and see setbacks as new beginnings.

**Work** with others towards a shared goal. This will allow you to achieve much more than if you were working alone. Be sure to create an environment that helps everyone bloom.

### MESSAGE

*Be bold with your next move. You are held in high regard and can afford to take risks.*

Joy comes to us
in moments –
ordinary moments.
We risk missing
out on joy when
we get too busy
chasing down the
extraordinary.

*Brené Brown*

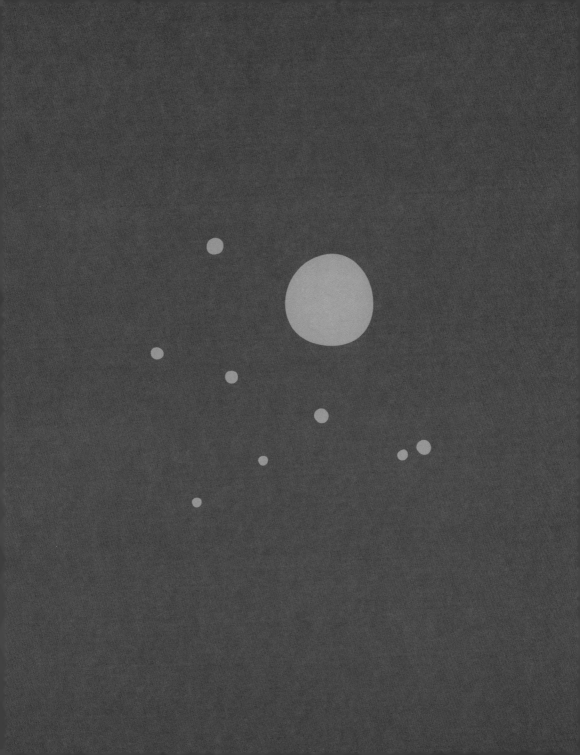

# Ladybird
## *New happiness is on its way*

**ESSENCE** *Loyal, curious and open-minded*

## SYMBOLISM

- Sacred blessings
- Quickness and alertness of mind
- Good fortune and luck
- The power of love
- Positive changes

## TEACHINGS

Ladybird as spirit animal teaches that a positive outlook can have a big impact. By being aware of the good things around you, you will create a happier and more fulfilling life. Be grateful, try to help or make other people smile, and seek out joy in every day.

## HOW TO RESPOND

**Find** meaning and value in whatever you do.

**Try** to do something good for someone else every day, whether that's offering a sympathetic ear to a friend or calling a family member you haven't talked to in a while.

**Surround** yourself with positive people. The company that you keep has a big impact on your attitude.

**Simplify** your life. Work out what's most important, and focus your time, energy and attention on these things.

**Seek out** new experiences so you're constantly learning and evolving.

## MESSAGE

*Joy is available to you in each moment if you know how to look for it.*

# Lion

## Take control of the situation

**ESSENCE** *Courage, strength and influence*

### SYMBOLISM

- An opportunity to lead
- Career success
- Protector of the weak
- Purity of heart
- Justice

### TEACHINGS

Lion as spirit animal instructs you to assert your authority and reclaim your power. Like Lion, do not bow to intimidation; instead stand your ground and meet any challenges head on. Be proud of the fact that you are a brave and fierce warrior with the ability to create your own destiny.

### HOW TO RESPOND

**Choose** your battles wisely. Not everything is worth fighting for, and sometimes it is better to simply walk away.

**Be prudent** by showing careful judgement when handling practical or delicate matters.

**Take** responsibility for your actions and own up when things go wrong.

**Look** out for friends or family in need of support. Simply reaching out can make a big difference to a person experiencing difficulties.

**Be quiet** as sometimes it's better to talk less and listen more. This will help you build stronger, deeper connections with others.

### MESSAGE

*Be tenacious: you can and will overcome life's obstacles and adversities.*

# Octopus

## Minimise drama in your life

ESSENCE *Purity, intelligence and mystery*

### SYMBOLISM

- Psychic ability
- Ability to hide in plain sight
- Hidden emotions
- Adaptability
- The power of focus

### TEACHINGS

When Octopus as spirit animal comes into your life, he teaches the skill of camouflage and disguise. Sometimes it is better to lay low and wait for a situation to unfold than to force a resolution. It may be time to hold your tongue and stay out of the drama.

### HOW TO RESPOND

**Reconsider** unhealthy relationships and commit to genuine, two-way friendships.

**Avoid** giving unsolicited advice and don't assume that you know best.

**Set** personal boundaries and reflect on what you truly feel, need and want out of life, both the big and small things.

**Spend** time alone. In a culture of oversharing, find authenticity in keeping some things sacred. Have a break from social media and take long walks in nature.

**Enjoy** watching from the sidelines. You don't always need to be in the thick of things.

### MESSAGE

*Learn that being authentic is to be yourself – it is not about proving yourself.*

Gratitude is the
wine for the soul.
Go on. Get drunk.

*Rumi*

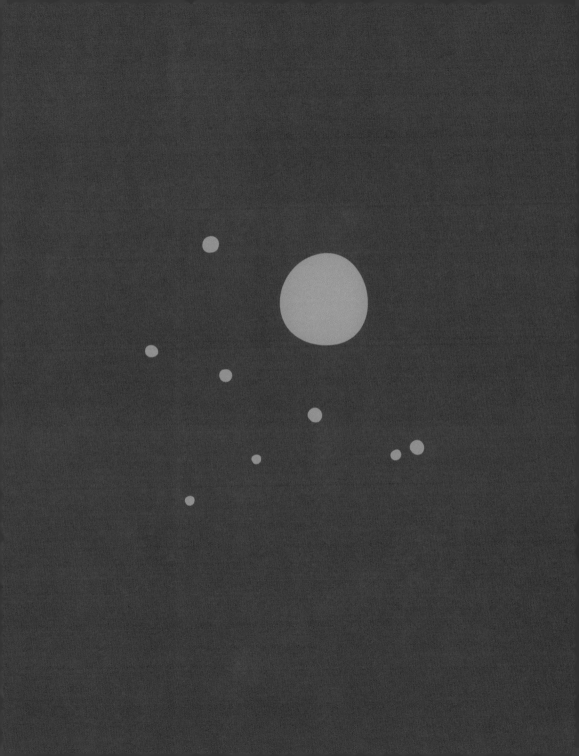

# Orangutan
*Find your place of peace*

ESSENCE *Playfulness, innocence and inquisitiveness*

## SYMBOLISM

- Healing past trauma
- Inner peace
- Self-sufficiency in a crisis
- Freedom from servitude
- Strong social bonds

## TEACHINGS

Just as Orangutan leads a solitary life in the forest, you too need a place where you can nourish your soul. Orangutan as spirit animal teaches that it is vital to refocus your mind and re-energise your spirit – it may be time to identify what brings you joy and what drains your energy.

## HOW TO RESPOND

**Work on** self-love and acceptance so you can reach out when you are in need.

**Cooperate** with others using diplomacy and tact. Sometimes it's better to step back and allow others to take charge.

**Honour** the most important women in your life by sending flowers or a card.

**Surround** yourself with nature. Feast on fruit, start a vegetable garden or invest in indoor plants.

**Avoid** social situations that make you feel uncomfortable. You don't need to say yes to every invitation.

## MESSAGE

*Act with integrity every day and stay away from people who are trying to drag you down.*

# Owl

## Look beyond the shadows on the horizon

**ESSENCE** *Wisdom, clairvoyance and resourcefulness*

### SYMBOLISM

- Ability to see through deception
- Gift of prophecy
- Guardian of honour
- Voyage into the unknown
- Spiritual protection

### TEACHINGS

Owl as teacher commands that you look fearlessly into the darkness to seek knowledge and truth on the other side. When Owl comes into your life as a spirit animal, it may be time to confront your fears: he teaches that the only way to move past them is to stare them down and win.

### HOW TO RESPOND

**Simplify** a task by breaking it down into smaller components and tackle them one by one to avoid being overwhelmed by the complexities.

**Use** the moon phases to set a monthly intention.

**Stop** and think. You'll have much better success if you plan out your strategies rather than rushing straight in.

**Wait** until night-time to tackle your most complex work. This is when your creative energies are at their strongest.

**Read** between the lines to understand what the universe is trying to tell you.

### MESSAGE

*Although the truth may be hard to accept, it's time to honestly examine the situation.*

# Peacock

*Be confident in your actions*

**ESSENCE** *Integrity, beauty and colour*

## SYMBOLISM

- Resurrection and rebirth
- Celebration of new life
- Royalty
- Human ego
- Drama based on past events

## TEACHINGS

Peacock as spirit animal teaches you to live a life of integrity and honour. When Peacock comes into your life, it's time to stand up for your values and hold firm to what you believe to be right and true. Now is the time to let your true colours shine through.

## HOW TO RESPOND

**Commit** to taking action. To succeed you'll need to maintain a delicate balance between confidence and humility.

**Pay** your good fortune forwards by treating someone to a cup of coffee, a meal or something bigger.

**Smile** to share your joy with the world. Simple actions can have a big impact.

**Invest** in experiences rather than 'things'. Material possessions will never bring true happiness; but gathering stories and memories will.

**Define** the change you want to see and identify the people who will support you in getting there.

## MESSAGE

*Once you commit to living your dreams, a completely new world will come into view.*

# Penguin
## *Create a powerful legacy*

---

**ESSENCE** *Pride, playfulness and self-discipline*

---

## SYMBOLISM

- Lovable nature
- Sense of responsibility
- Release of old beliefs
- Strong community networks
- An indomitable spirit

## TEACHINGS

Penguin as spirit animal teaches that you have the ability to thrive even in the hardest of conditions. Work out what you need to bring out the best in yourself and others, and stay true to that path. You have the skills to bring people together to create something special.

## HOW TO RESPOND

**Build** a strong community and happy family. These two things will carry you through life.

**Live** in the moment. Spend your time building powerful connections with others, creating beautiful art and cultivating your own spiritual growth.

**Use** stress to intensify your focus. Find inspiring mentors who have handled pressure and get them to show you how they operate.

**Communicate** as by talking to each other, we can challenge our thinking and always learn something new.

**Stay** lighthearted and use humour to make other people feel good.

---

## MESSAGE

*If you want to achieve success in anything, you must be consistent in your efforts.*

Not everything
that weighs you
down is yours
to carry.

*Juansen Dizon*

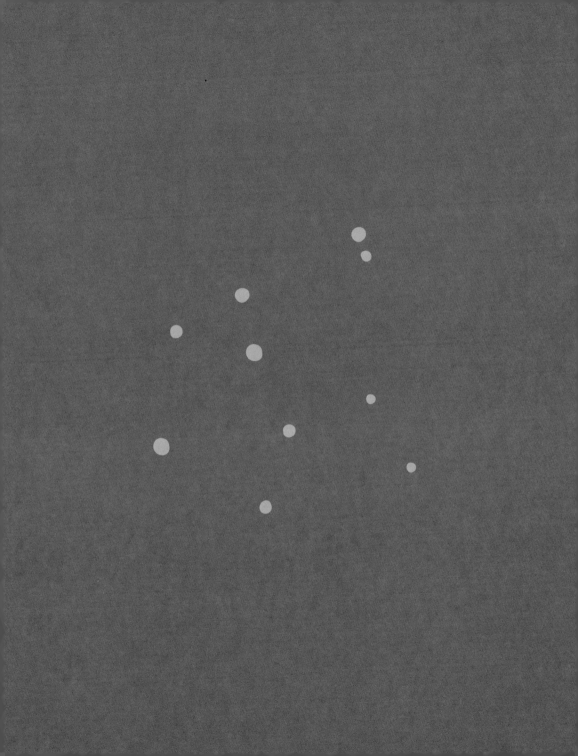

# Rabbit

*Fully embrace your creativity*

**ESSENCE** *Luck, vitality and light*

## SYMBOLISM

- Gift of abundance
- Fertility and procreation
- Vulnerability
- A strong sense of duty
- Guide to the spirit world

## TEACHINGS

Rabbit as spirit animal teaches that it is time to create the life of your dreams. When Rabbit comes into your life, you must utilise your abundant energy and act on your ideas and plans. You may need to think outside the box to find the right solutions for your needs.

## HOW TO RESPOND

**Look** before you leap. Although spontaneity is in your nature, don't act without first considering the potential consequences.

**Nourish** yourself with good food. Eating a plant-based diet will boost your health.

**Create** a fertile sacred space for your abundance to grow. This involves letting go of old beliefs, forgiving your mistakes and surrendering your fears.

**Be generous** to those around you. Give money to charity or fund a cause based on your passions

**Focus** on one thing at a time rather than jumping between projects.

## MESSAGE

*Overcome your fears and anxieties to create abundance at all levels of your life.*

# Snake

*Grow your confidence and self-esteem*

ESSENCE *Wisdom, change and longevity*

## SYMBOLISM

- Primal energy and life force
- Unconscious desire
- Life changes and transformation
- Sexual empowerment
- New beginnings

## TEACHINGS

The appearance of Snake spirit animal in your life means that exciting new opportunities are coming your way. Just like Snake sheds his skin, it's time to discard everything that's holding you back. Take this opportunity to identify poisonous or toxic people and remove them from your life.

## HOW TO RESPOND

**Stay** grounded by making decisions according to your beliefs and values, and don't be swayed by the opinions of others.

**Use** your charm and charisma to talk your way out of tricky situations.

**Be ready** for spiritual guidance. Unless you are open and receptive, change is not able to take place.

**Slow down** and beware of moving too fast into something that may not be quite right for you.

**Get rid** of what no longer serves you by dealing with challenging relationships that are weighing you down.

## MESSAGE

*Remain focussed and connect to the core of who you are in the face of uncertainty.*

# Spider
*Start on the path to freedom*

**ESSENCE** *Mystery, intricacy and patience*

## SYMBOLISM

- Feminine energy
- Life's ebb and flow
- Dark desires and seduction
- Financial gain
- Guidance from a higher power

## TEACHINGS

When Spider comes to you, it is a sign that it's time to weave your own destiny. Spider as spirit animal teaches that there is no point relying on others to shape your future; this is something that you and only you can do. It may be time to crawl out of your safety net.

## HOW TO RESPOND

**Watch** out for trickery or deceit in others.

**Get** some perspective so you can look at the situation from all angles. A health retreat or weekend away may give you the clarity you need.

**Wait** for the right time to share your news. Think about how it may affect others, and deliver your words carefully.

**Harness** your inner strength to get to where you need to be. You are formidable and brave.

**Don't see** your career or income as the sole measure of success.

## MESSAGE

*Let go of limiting beliefs so you can pursue the life you truly deserve.*

# Starfish

## Become who you were meant to be

---

**ESSENCE** *Colour, intrigue and happiness*

---

### SYMBOLISM

- Healing and renewal
- Infinite love
- Career advancement
- Patience in the face of adversity
- Great wisdom

### TEACHINGS

The appearance of Starfish as spirit animal is a reminder that being unique is better than being perfect. Starfish teaches that you must walk with your head held high and own who you were meant to be. When you learn to embrace your true self, the obstacles you are facing will start to fall away.

### HOW TO RESPOND

**Learn** to say no. This will help you overcome your fear of rejection and help you feel in control.

**Harness** the power of the ocean by walking on the beach, fossicking in tidal pools or swimming in the sea.

**Own** your idiosyncrasies. What makes you different also makes you interesting.

**Find** a new hobby if the monotony of daily life is leaving you unfulfilled. Trail hiking, calligraphy and photography are all excellent options.

**Throw** off others' expectations of you and live out your own dreams instead.

---

### MESSAGE

*Don't live to please others; allow your inner self to shine bright.*

# Swan

## Realise your own true beauty

**ESSENCE** *Elegance, balance and purity*

### SYMBOLISM

- Intuitive perception
- Separation from a loved one
- A bright future
- Divine blessings
- Inner and outer beauty

### TEACHINGS

The appearance of Swan as spirit animal means that it is time to shed your insecurities and self-doubts. Swan teaches that your future will be bright, but you must undergo a transformation before you get there. Learn from Swan gliding gracefully through the water – it's time for you to sink or swim.

### HOW TO RESPOND

**Have** compassion and view every aspect of yourself without judgement.

**Focus** on your health and fitness by moving your body every day.

**Look** beyond the present circumstances and imagine a brighter future. If you want happiness, fulfilment and inner peace, then believe that you have the power to achieve those things.

**Be open-minded** about the people you meet. Someone new will turn out to play an important role in your life.

**Feed** your intellect by joining a book club or library and reading a new book each month.

### MESSAGE

*Act with dignity and grace as you explore the path to unconditional self-acceptance.*

# Some people talk to animals. Not many listen though. That's the problem.

*A. A. Milne*

# Turtle

## Honour the natural rhythms of life

---

**ESSENCE** *Luck, patience and longevity*

---

### SYMBOLISM

- Completion of a project
- Bountiful harvest
- Ancient wisdom
- Freedom in mind and body
- A new lease of life

### TEACHINGS

When Turtle appears, he teaches that slow and steady will win the race. Do not rush to the quickest and easiest solution; take your time to appreciate the journey. Just as Turtle carries his home on his back, you too must learn to find peace wherever you are.

### HOW TO RESPOND

**Take** an early morning walk to help set your circadian rhythm and your focus for the day.

**Slow** your life down and live in the moment. Try turning off your computer, taking naps and cooking your meals from scratch.

**Honour** your emotions. Journalling is an excellent way to get in touch with your true feelings.

**Practise** mindful breathing to build resilience to stress, anxiety and anger.

**Find** a meaningful connection to nature by taking time to watch the rising and setting of the sun.

---

### MESSAGE

*Have faith that your intuition will guide you to where you need to be.*

# Wolf

*Find order out of chaos*

**ESSENCE** *Instinct, intelligence and power*

## SYMBOLISM

- Journey of self-discovery
- A thirst for freedom
- Social activism
- Loyalty and communication
- Intelligent teacher or muse

## TEACHINGS

When Wolf as spirit animal appears to you, it is time to act decisively regarding an important matter. Whether this is an issue at work, in your relationship or with friends, Wolf teaches that only you have the capacity to solve the problem. It may be time to step out of line.

## HOW TO RESPOND

**Claim** your personal power by acknowledging and declaring your ambition. You are wild and strong, and your actions should reflect this.

**Use** the full moon as a time for reflection and a chance to clear space for what you really want to attract in life.

**Accept** that life is short and time is precious, and act accordingly.

**Replace** negative self-talk with positive affirmations. Self-awareness is the first step to owning your power.

**Create** a sacred space to give you the chance to communicate with your higher self.

## MESSAGE

*Be bold – it's time to speak up and share your brilliance with the world.*

# Zebra

## Work diligently to achieve harmony

**ESSENCE** *Diplomacy, fairness and agility*

## SYMBOLISM

- Acceptance of differences
- A bold, brave life
- Strength in actions and words
- Liberation
- Opportunity for expansion

## TEACHINGS

Zebra as spirit animal teaches that you are an intrepid soul who must find purpose in life. Just as Zebra's stripes are perfectly balanced, his appearance reminds us that there are two sides to every story, and that your role is to navigate between them to create a harmonious resolution.

## HOW TO RESPOND

**Listen** carefully to what people are saying. Not everything is black and white, and sometimes you need to read between the lines.

**Share** your knowledge by mentoring or guiding others on the same path.

**Stay** independent and don't be swayed by others' opinions. They don't always have your best interests at heart.

**Set** your goals high. Yours will be a life of freedom once you find the right path.

**Embrace** your differences. Look for the beauty in others and remember that your way is not right for everyone.

## MESSAGE

*Be open to new ideas as these may set your life on a different course.*

HERRON

First Published in 2021 by Herron Book Distributors Pty Ltd
14 Manton St
Morningside
QLD 4170
www.herronbooks.com

Custom book production by Captain Honey Pty Ltd
12 Station Street
Bangalow
NSW 2479
www.captainhoney.com.au

Text copyright © Captain Honey Pty Ltd 2021

The publisher has made every effort to correctly identify authors of quotes. We apologise in advance for any unintentional errors or omissions and would be pleased to insert the appropriate credit in any subsequent edition of this book.

The moral right of the author has been asserted.

Cataloguing-in-Publication. A catalogue record for this book is available from the National Library of Australia

ISBN: 978-1-922432-17-9

Printed and bound in China

5 4 3 2 1    21 22 23 24 25